David

Scripture text from
The Contemporary English Version

Master
Books

CHAPTER 1

A Young Shepherd

The prophet Samuel pours oil on the head of young David to show that God has chosen David to become king. Samuel's eyes are raised to the heavens to ask that God bless David. The young boy lowers his head, a sign of respect for this honor. The colors used by the artist are simple and subdued. The architecture in the background shows the artist's taste for ancient times.

Felix Joseph Barrias, (1822-1907), Anointing of David by Samuel.

© Giraudon - Museum of Paris, Museum of the Little Palace, Paris (France).

Saul, the First King of Israel

The first king of Israel was chosen by the people more than 3000 years ago. He was named Saul. His rule began with great victories against the Philistine, enemies of Israel that lived along the coast of the Mediterranean Sea. But Saul became jealous of David because of his popularity among the people. Saul eventually considered him a threat and his own rival.

Saul's rule ended tragically in a battle against the Philistines on Mount Gilboa. At this time David was the leader of a group of men defending the villages against their enemy. David will soon replace Saul as the king of Israel.

Gelboe, Israel

"Human beings look at the face, but the Lord looks at the heart."

God Chooses David

The Bible tells how David was chosen king of Israel. The author wants to show that David is not a king like all others; David has been chosen by God. That is why God's representative Samuel* goes to look for the new king at Bethlehem.** In making his choice, Samuel does not consider physique, age, or strength but something that God alone knows: David's heart. Samuel anoints David in the name of the Lord God. David must wait, however, to become the new king until Saul is no longer ruling.

The Church of the Nativity at Bethlehem, the traditional site of Jesus' birth. Bethlehem was known as the City of David.

* Samuel
Samuel had a great influence in Israel. The people considered him a true prophet and man of God. Two books in the Christian Old Testament bear his name – 1 and 2 Samuel – though originally they made up a single book.

** Bethlehem
Bethlehem is a city of shepherds, situated about four miles south of Jerusalem. Bethlehem means "house" (Beth) "of bread" (lehem). Centuries later, Jesus will be born in this city.

3

God Looks at the Heart

1 Samuel 16.1-13 (extracts)

One day [The LORD] said, "Samuel, I've rejected Saul, and I refuse to let him be king any longer. Stop feeling sad about him. Put some olive oil in a small container and go visit a man named Jesse, who lives in Bethlehem. I've chosen one of his sons to be my king...."

"Tell everyone that you've come to offer ... a sacrifice to me, then invite Jesse to the sacrifice...."

Samuel did what the LORD told him and went to Bethlehem. The town leaders went to meet him, but they were terribly afraid and asked, "Is this a friendly visit?"

"Yes, it is!" Samuel answered.... Samuel also invited Jesse and his sons to come to the sacrifice, and he got them ready to take part.

When Jesse and his sons arrived, Samuel noticed Jesse's oldest son, Eliab. "He has to be the one the LORD has chosen," Samuel said to himself.

But the LORD told him, "Samuel, don't think Eliab is the one just because he's tall and handsome. He isn't the one I've chosen. People judge others by what they look like, but I judge people by what is in their hearts."

Jesse told his son Abinadab to go over to Samuel, but Samuel said, "No, the LORD hasn't chosen him...."

Jesse had all seven of his sons go over to Samuel. Finally, Samuel said, "Jesse, the LORD hasn't chosen any of these young men. Do you have any more sons?"

"Yes, Jesse answered. "My youngest son David is out taking care of the sheep."

"Send for him!" Samuel said. "We won't start the ceremony until he gets here."

Jesse sent for David. He was a healthy, good-looking boy with a sparkle in his eyes. As soon as David came, the LORD told Samuel, "He's the one! Get up and pour the olive oil on his head."

Samuel poured the oil on David's head while his brothers watched. At that moment, the Spirit of the LORD took control of David and stayed with him from then on.

Sacrifice

Samuel invites the people of Bethlehem to offer God the young calf that he brought with him. After the sacrifice a part of the meat of the victim is divided among the guests.

A Friendly Visit

In Hebrew, the language of the Bible, the word for a friendly visit is "peace," which is *shalom*. Even today this word serves as a greeting in Israel. The Arabs say *"salaam."*

The Spirit of the LORD

This expression signifies the wind, the breath, and the strength of the LORD who encourages and helps everyone to accomplish important actions.

The Heart vs. Appearance

Jealousy

People who are jealous cannot stand the thought that a neighbor, a friend, or anyone else would be more successful than they are. This is probably because they want (or need) to be loved and respected more than others. They are not satisfied with second place. They consider others as opponents who might take away some of their popularity or achievements. Jealous people are driven to use all means, good or bad, to do away with those they consider rivals.

Appearance

Many people these days are obviously influenced by popular magazines which show and promote looks and clothes as the means to success and popularity. Such people usually let themselves be enchanted by appearances, by the physique of the body, by expensive clothes, or by financial success. They expect themselves and others to look the same as the super model.

Heart

We say it is the "heart" that makes people act, that urges them to choose good or bad, that leads them to selfishness or the love of others, that brings them to be faithful to God or to turn away. The heart is "interior." It cannot be seen, yet it is the place where decisions and plans are secretly made.

Chosen by God

We call a person who is dedicated to living God's way in the world someone who is "chosen by God." Each of us, in fact, is chosen to live the way God intends for us to live. Each person, no matter how the exterior appearance looks, has been created by God to be a child of God. God chooses each one of us to work with other believers to make the world a more loving place.

Kings and Rulers

Kings and rulers who govern a country, a group, or a church have a serious responsibility. Their role consists in serving others, not in profiting from their position in order to gain personal wealth, privileges, or power. God wants them, above all, to put themselves at the service of others.

6

Opaque Screen

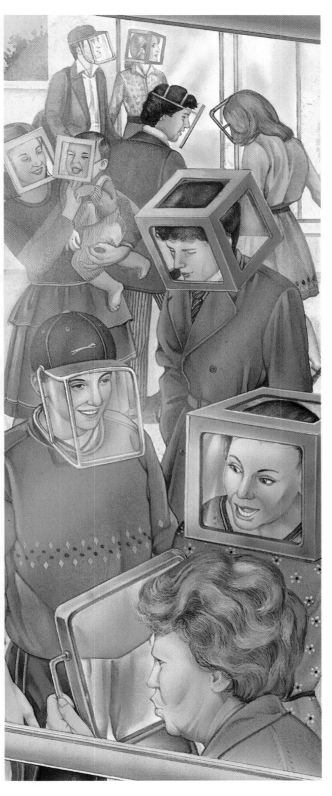

Very often people are judged according to their looks, their possessions, and their abilities.

Exterior appearances are like a dark screen. What is going on behind it in God's view?

God sees beneath the screen of appearances what is not visible in others at first glance.

God is not fooled by a strong or beautiful figure or by shining faces.

God looks at the heart!

For God, the only thing that counts is the beauty of the heart. This beauty is seen when we perform actions with love, when we share with the poor, when we struggle against evil, when we believe in God with full confidence and above all, when we are faithful in trials.

A French poet said, "What is essential is invisible to the eye."

The face can grow old and become ugly. It is the heart that makes human beings ageless, strong and beautiful.

CHAPTER 2

An Unusual Battle

This artist, a student and imitator of Caravaggio, shows David glowing with light. All the faces of the people are bright and full of depth. In spite of his youth, David proudly holds in one hand the head of Goliath, the Philistine giant he has just defeated and killed.

Manfredi Bartolomeo, (1582 to about 1622), David Triumphant

© Giraudon - Louvre Museum, Paris (France)

The Philistine Danger

The sea, seen from Haifa in Israel

King Saul ruled for forty years. He fought several battles against the Philistines who were trying to take over part of Israel's territories. These warriors were young, well-armed men who had come by way of the sea and knew how to make strong weapons. Samson the Judge had already fought them in earlier times.

Saul was acquainted with David. He even arranged for his daughter Michal to marry David. Saul's son Jonathan* was David's faithful friend. Yet Saul was still afraid that David would take his place as king, and he tried several times to kill David. He was never successful.

A Philistine

Who Will Accept the Challenge?

How did Saul become acquainted with David? The books of Samuel give no explanation. Saul was out fighting against the Philistines. David's three older brothers, Eliab, Abinadab, and Shammah were fighting in Saul's army. One day David went to the army camp to take food to his brothers and found the soldiers terrified. Why?

Every morning, Goliath** the Philistine champion, a giant of a man who was dressed in armor and armed with weapons, approached Saul's army camp and cried out, *"Choose your best soldier to come out and fight me! If he can kill me, our people will be your slaves. But if I kill him, your people will be our slaves."* The Israelites trembled with fear, and not one of them was brave enough to take up Goliath's challenge. When David saw this, he went up to Saul and said, *"I'll go out and fight him myself!"*

* Jonathan
Saul's son Jonathan was a close friend of David. Jonathan died with his father in the battle at Gilboa. David was filled with grief and composed a song that tells of their deaths: "How could they have fallen, these heroes, in the midst of the battle?" (2 Samuel 1.19-25)

** Goliath
According to 1 Samuel 17.4, this Philistine warrior was over nine feet tall. He had a bronze helmet and wore armor that weighed 176 pounds. The blade of his lance alone weighed twenty pounds.

David and Goliath

1 Samuel 17.40-51 (extracts)

[David] picked up his shepherd's stick. He went out to a stream and picked up five smooth rocks and put them in his leather bag. Then with his sling in hand, he went straight toward Goliath....

When Goliath saw that David was just a healthy, good-looking boy, he made fun of him. "Do you think I'm a dog?" Goliath asked. "Is that why you've come after me with a stick?..."

David answered:

You've come out to fight me with a sword and a spear and a dagger. But I've come out to fight you in the name of the LORD All-Powerful....

When Goliath started forward, David ran toward him. He put a rock in his sling and swung the sling around by its straps. When he let go of one strap, the rock flew out and hit Goliath on the forehead. It cracked his skull, and he fell facedown on the ground....

David ran over and pulled out Goliath's sword. Then he used it to cut off Goliath's head.

When the Philistines saw what had happened to their hero, they started running away.

Shepherd

David was a shepherd. He knew how to defend his flock against wild animals. Later he will be the king and shepherd of his people.

The LORD All-Powerful

This expression (in Hebrew, *Yahweh Sabaoth*) means "God of the armies." It concerns the heavenly armies, the stars. Sometimes it is translated as "the LORD of Hosts."

Running Away

When the enemy runs away, the women of Israel celebrate the victory with singing and dancing. Thus they provoke Saul's jealousy.

The Strength of the Weak

The Powerful

Some people with power do evil things. They flex their muscles to impress people. They show off their wealth by buying more and more. They boast about their privileges and their high places in society. They mistreat or oppress others. They despise the humble. They are proud and like to think of themselves as dictators.

Fear

The powerful sometimes cause us fear. How can anyone not be afraid of what they are able to do with their power? They have the ability to make laws and impose their own desires on everyone else. It seems better to bow before them in obedience rather than challenge them and get into trouble? It makes good sense to be on their side rather than to stand up against them.

The Weak

Those who are weak lack riches and are rarely recognized by the public. They must be satisfied with what they have and with who they are. They are denied the right to speak out and to make decisions. They usually face some kind of oppression and sometimes are deprived of nourishment. If they are foreigners, they are held in contempt. They hunger and thirst for justice and for happiness!

Hope

Hope gives strength to the oppressed. They trust that one day they will be able to recover their dignity. They believe that the powerful, with their scorn and their pride, will not always win. Trusting in God, they are not overcome but strive patiently to be respected. They want nothing more than to have the same rights and privileges as other people.

God Is on the Side of the Weak

God is never on the side of the proud and powerful. Over and over in the Bible we read how God upholds and strengthens the weak. He gives them courage to resist oppression and hope that someday their situation will be different.

Winners

Great
is the strength of the humble,
for they count on God
who comes to their aid
in their weakness.

They have overcome hatred
by closing their hearts
to revenge.
They overcome violence
by refusing to return blows!

They overcome offenses
by keeping their hands open
in pardon and being ready for dialogue.
They overcome selfishness
by organizing to share.
They overcome anger
by answering with meekness!

They are winners
in never giving up their efforts.
They are winners
because they pledge
never to be conquered!

They overcome evil
by relying on God!
They are winners
because with all their heart
and with all their strength,
they rely on God
and on their neighbor!

CHAPTER • 3

A Joyful Dance

In a copper etching, this Swiss artist shows David dancing and playing the harp as he walks in front of the Sacred Chest of the Agreement. The people in the procession are joyful and happy as they celebrate a victory. Reds and bright greens reinforce the joyful atmosphere of this painting. The many musical instruments show the importance of music and dancing during this period.

Matthew Merian the Elder, (1593-1650), David Dancing before the Sacred Chest of the Agreement

© Photo AKG Paris (France) - Kunsthandel, Berlin (Germany)

A New Capital

Carved model representing ancient Jerusalem

After the death of Saul, David became king. He chose as his capital the city of Jerusalem*, occupied by Jebusites, native dwellers of the country. David easily conquered them and took control of the city. David's choice of Jerusalem was very clever – it was centrally located and had belonged to non-Israelites. Therefore, no tribe could claim it as their own.

From his capital in Jerusalem, David was able to unite the northern and the southern tribes of Israel. After 3000 years, Jerusalem still exists.

A Religious Center

Tavant, crypt of Saint Nicholas Church. David Dancing, twelfth century.
© Telarci – Giraudon/French Monument Museum, Paris, (France)

From the time of Moses to the time of David, the Israelites looked to the Sacred Chest of the Agreement as the sign of God's presence among them. The Sacred Chest was movable and often sheltered under a tent. This was practical because the people frequently moved from place to place. Now that Israel had a permanent land, it seemed right that the Sacred Chest would also have a permanent resting place. Naturally, that place would be Jerusalem. David had a special place** prepared with a tent to keep the Chest. He brought it to Jerusalem with much fanfare and celebration. With the Sacred Chest in Jerusalem, this capital city also became the religious center of David's kingdom.

* Jerusalem
In Hebrew, Jerusalem means "city of peace."

** Special place
Later, at this same place, David will buy a piece of land and build an altar there. This is the site where the Temple will later be built.

Jerusalem today

15

The Ark at Jerusalem

2 Samuel 6.12-19 (extracts)

David went to Obed Edom's house to get the chest and bring it to David's City. Everyone was celebrating…. He was dancing for the LORD with all his might, but he wore only a linen cloth. He and everyone else were celebrating by shouting and blowing horns while the chest was being carried along.

Saul's daughter Michal looked out her window and watched the chest being brought into David's city. But when she saw David jumping and dancing for the LORD, she was disgusted.

They put the chest inside a tent that David had set up for it. David worshiped the LORD by sacrificing animals and burning them on an altar, then he blessed the people in the name of the LORD All-Powerful. He gave all the men and women in the crowd a small loaf of bread, some meat, and a handful of raisins, and everyone went home.

Obed Edom

The Sacred Chest of the Agreement was returned after being captured by the Philistines. It was placed in the house of a man with a foreign name. *Obed-Edom* means "the servant of Edom." God had blessed his house.

He Was Dancing

In Israel people dance a lot, at weddings, on popular holidays and at wine-harvesting, but also at religious celebrations. Dancing is considered a way for the body to pray.

Michal

David's wife criticized him after the celebration, "Why did you expose yourself today before the servants?" David answered, "It is before the LORD that I danced."

Feasting and Dancing

Sacrifices

Many people think that offering sacrifices to God means giving things to God or fasting (going without eating). But isn't it better to offer God our love? We offer our love by trusting and praying to God, and by obeying the command to others.

Signs of Presence

Churches and temples are signs of God's presence in the midst of people. But another important sign of God's presence are human beings themselves — men and women of all cultures and ethnic backgrounds. All are created in the image of God and God's love can work through them to touch others.

Dancing

Words are sometimes not enough when we experience overwhelming joy. Words cannot always express happiness that is bubbling over! When troubles are forgotten and God's glory is deeply felt, it is natural for us to dance for joy!

Celebrate

Throughout the year, Christians regularly come together to praise and celebrate God. They are thankful for God's faithful love and show their love as God's children in response. They celebrate the fact that God gives them life.

Sharing

When Christians come together to celebrate their joy in trusting God, it is important for them also to remember their brothers and sisters in distress. Celebrating God requires believers to work together to share the earth so that all people may join in the celebration.

Jerusalem

Jerusalem is much more than the capital city of the modern nation of Israel. Jerusalem is also a place of heritage for millions of people. So much hope was born in this city. It is the place where agreements were made and renewed between God and God's people. Events happened here that truly turned the world upside down!

For some time, the holy city has been a place of strife and fighting, with Jews and Arabs wanting control. God's prophets proclaimed that one day, Messiah will come to establish peace.

The violence in the city is hard to stop, because of hatred in people's hearts and minds. There has always been a struggle over Jerusalem, for God has chosen it as his dwelling place and those who oppose him try to prevent his will from being done. One day, though, God will say, Enough! He alone will bring lasting peace to this city and to the entire world, and Jerusalem will be a place where people from all nations will gather to worship the one, true God. What a day that will be!

Strange Promises

This French artist combines strength and gentleness in the faces of the two figures. Conscious of the importance of the moment, David sits before Nathan the prophet. Nathan announces the agreement that God makes with David and with his descendants. The two men are calm and full of hope.

Jean Colombe (died in 1529), "Splendid Hours of the Duke of Berry" Psalm 31, David and Nathan (ms. 65/1284 fol. 65 v) end of the fifteenth century.

© Giraudon - Conde Museum, Chantilly (France)

A Dynasty

The Judean desert

David is considered the greatest king of Israel. He extended the borders* of his kingdom and organized the government. He also founded a dynasty, a family of kings. All the kings who would reign at Jerusalem for four centuries (from 970 to 587 B.C.) would be descendants of David. The Lord did not allow David, however, to build the Temple.**

A New Period of Growth

Throughout the history of Israel, solemn agreements (covenants) between God and the people are made. In the days of Noah, God made an agreement with all creation never to destroy the world with the flood again. Later God made an agreement with Abraham that he would have innumerable descendants and that they would be given their own land. At the time of Moses, God made an agreement with the Hebrew people who had escaped from Egypt.

By the time of King David, these agreements are far in the past. So many things have changed in Israel. The people are no longer nomads but live in a land of their own. They are no longer divided but have a king. The agreements and promises need to be renewed.

Nathan is the prophet sent to announce God's agreement (covenant) with David. This begins a new period in Israel's history. God makes an agreement with David and his descendants that they would always rule in Jerusalem. The text on the following page is the most important in David's history.

Alliance, statue from New Orleans in the United States

* Borders
Throughout Israel's history, the country had never been so extensive as it was during David's rule. See the map on page 35.

** Temple
David's son Solomon will build the Temple at Jerusalem. The Temple was known as the House of God, the place where God was among the Israelites.

Section of a model of Jerusalem

Nathan's Prophecy

2 Samuel 7. 2-18 (excerpts)

As David was talking with Nathan the prophet, David said, "Look around! I live in a palace made of cedar, but the sacred chest has to stay in a tent."

Nathan replied, "The LORD is with you, so do what you want!"

That night the LORD told Nathan to go to David and give him this message:

David, you are my servant, so listen to what I say. Why should you build a temple for me?… I brought you in from the fields where you took care of sheep, and I made you the leader of my people. Wherever you went, I helped you…

Now I promise that you and your descendants will be kings. I'll choose one of your sons to be king when you reach the end of your life and are buried in the tomb of your ancestors. I'll make him a strong ruler, and no one will be able to take his kingdom away from him. He will be the one to build a temple for me. I will be his father and he will be my son….

But I will never put an end to my agreement with him, as I put an end to my agreement with Saul, who was king before you. I will make sure that one of your descendants will always be king….

David went into the tent he had set up for the sacred chest. Then he sat there and prayed:

LORD, All-Powerful, my family and I don't deserve what you have already done for us.

Nathan

Nathan is a prophet who plays an important role in David's life when things are going well (as here) and also when things are going badly (as in the next chapter).

You And Your Descendants

In this sentence the LORD promises to build David a "house." That house refers to David's descendants who will rule Israel as kings.

Temple

A second meaning of the word "house" in this conversation is the Temple which David's son Solomon will build for the LORD.

Renewal

Agreement

An agreement between two peoples or groups of people means that they are bound and obligated to live up to the terms of the agreement. This may mean living together in peace, obeying certain rules or guidelines, or helping one another in times of difficulties. God

made an agreement with the people of Israel out of love for them to be the special people of God. He has saved them from countless dangers. Never will God abandon us to the powers of evil. In return, God demands that we be faithful to how he intends us to live.

Promises

God's promises are always kept. God can be trusted to be faithful. How faithful are we in keeping our promises to God and to others? We promise several things: to use our God-given talents to grow in God's image and likeness; to respond to God's love by loving God and others; to show our concern for those who suffer from poverty and sickness and physical conditions. Do we keep these promises?

Fresh Promises

It is difficult to keep every promise we make. Little by little daily problems distract us. Slowly monotony washes away our good intentions. That is why it is important at regular times, both in the privacy of our heart and in public with other believers, to renew the promises we have made to the Lord. We want to be faithful every day of our life.

Reminder

In order not to forget the promises we made in our agreements with God, we need encouragement. Other people remind us of our promise to love God by their prayer life, by their own praise of God, and by their writings. By word and action, but above all, by the gift of themselves in serving the most neglected, others remind us of our promise to love others as demanded in our agreement with God.

Listening

To remain faithful to the agreement with God, it is necessary to listen. To learn the art of listening, we must turn to God each day in prayer. We need to be attentive and recognize the signs God sends us quietly through people and through events, both small and large. We need to be conscious of the things God asks of us in the Bible and put into practice the words we read there.

Daily Agreement

The agreement between
God and humanity
is not an event of the past.
Each day, each moment,
God renews his promises!

For suffering humanity,
for starving humanity,
for humanity struggling to bring peace
where there is conflict,
for humanity working for
the advancement of science
and the common good,
for humanity freeing itself from
the forces of evil,
for humanity striving for unity,
for humanity struggling against the bonds
of selfishness,
for humanity striving
with all its energies
to resemble God,
for humanity concerned
with living faithful
to the promises of the agreement.

For to all humanity,
each day,
consciously and deliberately,
God pledges the help
of his love and
his presence!

CHAPTER 5

A Fault Pardoned

This detail of the tapestry of the Davanzatii Palace at Florence (Italy) represents Bathsheba in her garden, preparing for a bath. She is accompanied by her two maids. The realism of the drapery is accentuated by the play of lights and shadows.

Made in Flanders (the tapestry), The story of David and Bathsheba: David sees Bathsheba

© Scala - Davanzati Palace, Florence (Italy)

Good and Bad

Amman in Jordan

In David, as in every other human being, there is both good and bad. The Bible does not hide the weaknesses of the famous king. This is surprising because these pages were written by the royal scribes.* How could they speak of the bad in their ruler? Perhaps it was because they recognized that no one – even a king – is perfect besides God.

David and Bathsheba

Second Samuel includes the familiar story of David and Bathsheba. Israel's army is on a campaign under the direction of General Joab. The troops are besieging the city of Rabbah.** David, however, remains in Jerusalem.

During his afternoon rest on the terrace of his palace, David notices a woman bathing nearby. She is very beautiful, so the king inquires who she is. He is told the woman is Bathsheba, the wife of Uriah the Hittite. David sends for her and falls in love with her. To cover his sin of taking another man's wife, he writes a letter to General Joab: "Put Uriah up front in the battle and retreat behind him." His directions are obeyed and Uriah is killed before the walls of Rabbah. In the midst of such an injustice, the prophet Nathan cannot be silent.

Bathsheba goes into mourning for her dead husband. When the time for mourning is over, David brings her to the palace, and she becomes his wife. She bears a son who dies at birth. The second son will be named Solomon, who will later become David's successor as king.

History

Statue of a royal scribe
© Egyptian Museum of Cairo, (Egypt)

* Scribes
It was perhaps the court scribes during the rule of David or Solomon that recorded many of the events during the kingship of David.

** Rabbah
This is the capital city of the Ammonites who lived across the Jordan River from Israel. The city still stands today as Ammon, the capital of Jordan. See the map on page 35.

You Are the Man!

2 Samuel 12.1-13 (extracts)

The LORD... sent Nathan the prophet to tell this story to David:

A rich man and a poor man lived in the same town. The rich man owned a lot of sheep and cattle, but the poor man had only one little lamb that he had bought and raised. The lamb became a pet for him and his children. He even let it eat from his plate and drink from his cup and sleep on his lap. The lamb was like one of his own children.

One day someone came to visit the rich man, but the rich man didn't want to kill any of his own sheep or cattle and serve it to the visitor. So he stole the poor man's little lamb and served it instead.

David was furious with the rich man and said to Nathan, "I swear by the living LORD that the man who did this deserves to die!"

... Then Nathan told David:

You are that rich man! Now listen to what the LORD God of Israel says to you: "I chose you to be the king of Israel. I kept you safe from Saul and even gave you his house... Why did you disobey me and do such a horrible thing? You murdered Uriah the Hittite... so you could take his wife.

... David said, "I have disobeyed the LORD."

... Nathan answered... "He has forgiven you, and you won't die."

Tell This Story

The prophet begins by telling a story, a parable. David thinks the main character is someone else and condemns him sharply.

Disobeyed

David is not proud. He recognizes his sin. One of the psalms shows David's attitude: "Have pity on me, O God, in your goodness, in your great tenderness wipe out my guilt!"

Forgiven

David had said that the thief who took the lamb merited death. David merited it as well. But God says to him, "You will not die."

Each One

Mixture

Good and bad are present in each human being. It is not as if perfect people stand on one side and sinners on the other. Every person falls into sin at times and at other times resists evil and obeys God's commandments.

Both actions are decided in the heart, the place where we choose secretly and freely how we will act: either to allow evil to control us or to fight evil with the love of God and others.

Deprived

Many people in the world are deprived of possessions and freedom. They live in poverty and under the oppression of unjust economic and political systems. Such evil systems are concerned primarily with money and power.

Accusations

There is a general tendency in people to lay responsibility for the ills of society upon others. Thus others are blamed for the growing delinquency among youth, for the lack of job opportunities, and for other evils in society. Sometimes we wonder whether others are capable of anything besides evil. But we need to look within ourselves. Is it always true that the fault lies with others?

It Is You

We can all admit that we sometimes allow and contribute to the growth of evil in our world. We can also admit that it is I who can allow selfishness to become my master. It is I who must put an end to its growth in myself and in others.

Remembering Sinfulness

The first requirement for overcoming evil is to recognize the place it has in our lives. We must start with our own conversion toward the ways of God. It is important first to turn to God to acknowledge our sinfulness. God does not force anything on us – even the love that helps us live according to God's intention – but God waits for us to admit our failures. Then God comes quickly and generously to assist us in our desire to do good.

One Heart with God

One heart with God,
in spite of his imperfections,
David has been named
"according to God's heart!"
He was not pure,
he was not just,
he was not good
entirely.

All who
are friends of God
are called to be
"according to God's heart."

It is not necessary
for them to be perfect,
but they need to speak and act
as children of God.

It is up to them to try
all day long, to overcome the evil
that knocks at their heart.
It is up to them
to drive out the powerful
who are depriving the poor
of their dignity and rights.

In order to be "according
to God's heart,"
there is one road only:
to listen to the Gospel,
and to speak and act
as Jesus,
the Son of God, did.

David Remembered

Saul, the unfortunate king, has quickly been forgotten. But the memory of David has been kept through the ages. Even today people remember his strong rule in early Israel.

The Psalms of David

David danced and also played the harp. Saul asked David repeatedly to play the harp to calm his nerves. David also composed songs of praise or psalms. The biblical book of Psalms contains 150 psalms or songs. Of these, 73 are attributed to David.

These psalms did not remain in a drawer or on library shelves.

Michelangelo's David at Florence in Italy

Throughout history they have been sung – by the Jews and by Christians. Even today, in synagogues, churches, and monasteries, the psalms are heard in many languages. Some of these are very familiar: *"You, LORD, are my shepherd"* (Psalm 23.l) or *"From a sea of troubles I call out to you, LORD"* (Psalm 130.1) or *"Shout the LORD's praises in the highest heavens"* (Psalm 148.1).

Musical Angel, Western side of the Strasbourg Cathedral

A New David

The kingdom of David and of his successors lasted about four centuries. In 587 B.C., everything collapsed. The people of Israel were taken into exile by the Babylonian armies. Kingship disappeared from Israel, but the memory of David remained alive. When life was hard in exile under foreign occupation or in poverty, the people longed for the great King David. They remembered the promise God had made to David and his descendants that their rule would never end. They began to hope for the return of another king like David. They believed that like David this new king would also be anointed by God to rule Israel. They expected the coming of "the anointed one" would rescue them from oppression. In Hebrew, the word that means "the anointed one" is "the Messiah." In Greek, the word is "the Christ."

Centuries later the people continued to wait. They wondered: "Will the Messiah ever come? What will he do when he does? Will he free our country from Roman occupation? Will he establish peace and justice on earth?"

Jesus Son of David

Jesus was born among the people who were waiting for the Messiah who would free them from Roman oppression. Throughout the public ministry of Jesus, some people would ask: "Is Jesus the Messiah we've been waiting for?"

Christ in the Church of Saint Savior in Chora, in Istanbul (Turkey)

For the earliest Christians, the answer is clear. Jesus is the new David, the Messiah, the Christ. That is why they called him Jesus the Christ sent from God.

Two of the Gospel writers in particular speak of Jesus as the son of David. When the angel announces the birth of Jesus to Mary, he says that the Lord God will *"make him king, as his ancestor David was"* (Luke 1.32). In Matthew's Gospel, the genealogy of Jesus begins with the words, *"Jesus Christ came from the family of King David"* (Matthew 1.1). Jesus was born *"in King David's hometown"* of Bethlehem (Luke 2.11). When people asked Jesus to heal them, they shouted *"Son of David, have pity on us!"* (Matthew 9.27). And when Jesus enters Jerusalem, the crowd cries aloud: *"Hooray for the Son of David!"* (Matthew 21.9).

A world where we will be happier.

More than David

But Jesus did not come to rebuild or remake what David had made. He did not come to build a kingdom that would be under his administration, his officials, his soldiers, and his wars. He did not come for his own well being. Nor did he come only for the poor of Judea. Jesus expands the kingdom of David. He came to fulfill God's plan for a world of justice and peace for all people. By his example Jesus sowed the seeds of love. Through his Spirit, he still helps us today to build a world ruled not by power but by humility and love and happiness. For Christians, Jesus is not only the "son of David" but also the "Son of God."

Titles already published:

Creation — When God Made the World.

Abraham and His Family — A Man of Faith

Moses — The Deliverance of Israel and God's Commands

The Promised Land — From Joshua to the First Leaders of Israel

Solomon — A Man of Wisdom

The Childhood of Jesus — Born to Save the World

Jesus Calls — Come, and Be Fishers of Men

Jesus Heals — The Faith That Heals

Who Is Jesus? — Son of God, Son of Man

The Mission of Jesus — Good News for Everyone

The Parables of Jesus — The Teachings of Jesus

Forthcoming titles in the JUNIOR BIBLE Collection:

- The First Prophets
- Passion and Resurrection
- Exile and Return
- Isaiah, Micah, Jeremiah
- Jesus and the Outcasts
- Jesus in Jerusalem
- Acts
- Wisdom
- Psalms
- Women
- Revelation
- Letters

David's Kingdom

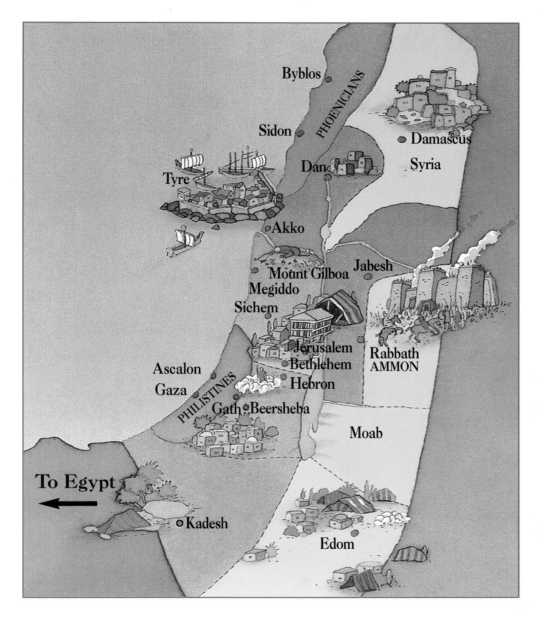

 David's kingdom

Countries conquered by David

David

ORIGINAL TEXT BY

Joan Marie BOEHLE, OSU,

Loretta PASTVA, SND,

Albert HARI, Charles SINGER

ENGLISH TEXT ADAPTED BY

the American Bible Society

PHOTOGRAPHY

Frantisek ZVARDON

ILLUSTRATORS

Mariano VALSESIA, Betti FERRERO

MIA. Milan Illustrations Agency

LAYOUT

Bayle Graphic Studio

FIRST PRINTING: NOVEMBER 2000

Copyright © 2000 by Master Books
for the CBA U.S. edition.

For information write: Master Books, P.O. Box 727, Green Forest, AR 72638.

ISBN: 0-89051-329-5

Master Books

ÉDITIONS DU SIGNE

© ÉDITIONS DU SIGNE 1998